THE CARE AND PRESERVATION OF
PHILATELIC MATERIALS

THE CARE AND PRESERVATION OF

PHILATELIC
MATERIALS

T. J. Collings and R. F. Schoolley-West

THE BRITISH LIBRARY

Note: Readers who wish to receive further information on current suppliers of conservation materials are asked to write to the authors, c/o Philatelic Collections, The British Library, 14 Store Street, London WC1.

Front cover: Stamps stuck down with glue, spoiling both stamps and album.

First published 1989 by
The British Library
Great Russell Street
London WC1B 3DG

British Library Cataloguing in Publication Data
Collings, T. J.
   The care and preservation of philatelic materials.
   1. Postage stamps. Preservation
   I. Title   II. Schoolley-West, R. F.   III. British Library
   769.56

ISBN 0 7123 0136 4

Designed by Andrew Shoolbred
Printed in England by Henry Ling, The Dorset Press, Dorchester and York House Graphics, Hanwell, Middlesex

Contents

Preface

Over the years serious collectors have always handled their stamps with care, but perhaps without awareness of the need to practise good preservation techniques; nor indeed did many aspire to the degree of knowledge necessary to do more than guard against the more evident hazards.

With regard to the less obvious precautions necessary for long-term preservation – the use of acid-free materials, for example, or the requirements related to temperature, humidity and exposure to light, and projection against rubbing – the only sources of information for the collector have been occasional articles in the pages of philatelic magazines.

It was in a paper presented to the British Philatelic Federation Congress at Norwich in 1986 that Bob Schoolley-West – drawing on his outstandingly good work with the British Library Philatelic Collections – outlined the hazards and spoke of the serious need for awareness of harmful materials and techniques. He has now followed that up by collaborating with Tom Collings in producing this book. Tom Collings is well-known in the conservation field for his expertise in the preservation of photographic images and printed material, and for his knowledge of specialist papers. In addition he has published work on a range of conservation subjects.

In the past there has been no concerted attempt to make the collector aware of the need for good preservation practice. This book, the first of its kind to be published, fills that gap more than adequately.

The book will be most useful for those who are concerned for the future and who wish to learn more about the somewhat complex problems involved. They will then at least be aware of the questions to be asked when considering the leaves, mounting materials and containers which may safely be used in connection with their collections.

If due attention is given to the advice in the pages of this book, collectors in the future will look on the measures taken now as one reason for their being able still to take great pleasure from the material which we so much value and enjoy today.

John B. Marriott, LVO, RDP, FRPSL

Introduction

Whether aged eight or eighty, a collector with a few stamps, envelopes and postcards in a biscuit tin or a curator responsible for a national philatelic collection, everyone has a responsibility to keep his or her collection in the best manner to ensure that the individual items are preserved as well as possible. This book is designed to be a preservation guide for those responsible for stamps and other philatelic material. It provides the necessary technical background to the simple methods recommended for the long term preservation of a collection. It does not instruct on restoration techniques but aims to create a general awareness of what is required for the good housekeeping of a collection, and indicates bad as well as good preservation practices.

It is only in recent times that collectors of philatelic materials have taken an interest in preservation, whilst other areas of collectables have traditionally been concerned with it for many years. If one considers the long collecting tradition for furniture, fine art, books, prints and other complex items, all of which, in terms of collecting interest, have a much longer history than philately, one might expect that the preservation problems associated with these collections would be far greater than those of a philatelic nature. This is, in fact, not the case due to the small size and large numbers of individual philatelic items, and their paper base which means that damage occurs more easily. In addition, their complex nature means that interactions of the fundamental constituents have to be considered. The inks, both printing as well as writing, adhesives, pigments, dyes, phosphors, plastics and papers which have been used at various times and in different countries give an initial indication of the wide range of materials which have to be taken into account. It is also important to appreciate that the objects themselves have never been produced to have more than a limited life.

It is fortunate that much of the knowledge acquired over many years relating to the preservation of other objects may, in many cases, be applied to philatelic materials. However, particular combinations of materials do not necessarily occur in these other objects so their specific properties have had to be deduced. Further, the more recent work carried out into the preservation of photographic materials assists in making recommendations relating to the care of philatelic materials which have some photographic content. Traditionally, in philately, most collectors handle their material carefully and as a result of this practice in the past, examples of virtually anything which has been produced are available in varying degrees of preservation and are still available for the collector. But more than good handling is necessary if our philatelic heritage is to be preserved for the future.

In general terms the combination of these various factors present the problems which confront the collector today. If future generations are to continue to gain pleasure and knowledge from the material which is collected, it can be only as the result of good preservation techniques being practised now.

Preservation, it must be emphasised, is not the sole responsibility of museums and county or state archives, but should be practised by any person holding the material, including the private collector, even though the material may be in his or her care for a relatively short period. Most collectors do not have the resources available to them to set up a 'museum' type environment, but with reasonable care and a few simple techniques involving relatively little expense quite a lot may be achieved. Just as important, collectors without experience in the more complex preservation techniques should not attempt to undertake them, as irreversible damage to the material can result or unnecessary deterioration be induced. Certainly no techniques involving repair or enhancement should be employed as these are not philatelically acceptable and require expert opinion as to their desirability.

Whilst most items within a collection are usually in good condition, the same cannot be said for 'crash' items. Items which have, for example, survived a plane crash or boat sinking, may have been subjected to the effects of fire and smoke, or fresh or sea water. As such, they will already have deteriorated more than usual, and very careful conservation is essential.

Preservation of materials is concerned with the elimination, in part or total, of the various factors which threaten the continuing existence of an item in its present form. This will include ensuring that the material is not introduced to new harmful substances and situations. These factors fall into several categories, not the least of which are the harmful components of the material itself: the degrading content of many papers and additives or coatings applied to them including certain inks and dyes and the destructive effectives of some adhesives. All other factors involve outside interference with the material, either occurring naturally, such as the atmosphere, fire, flood or infestation by insects and micro-organisms, or introduced by man in storage, handling and usage of the items. The development of plastics and other modern materials and their use in virtually every area of life today means that the philatelist can benefit from them, but only if the correct ones are selected. Our constantly changing way of life may also have an effect upon the condition of material at some time in the future and because of this there can be no hard and fast rules laid down. Much of what can be recommended can never be more than a compro-mise. The careful application and appreciation of the techniques given in this book will assist in the considerable extension of the life of items in collections today, but regrettably it must be accepted that collections will continue to deteriorate as they have done since they were first produced. This insidious deterioration cannot be stopped, though all have a responsibility to slow it down as much as possible.

Factors affecting permanence

A number of factors have to be fully understood before there can be any chance of success in preserving an object. The complexity and number of these factors is dependent upon the nature of the materials involved. The problem is that, when dealing with mat-erials which are naturally occurring and organic in nature, there are no fixed compositions, so that making decisions and recommendations is often very difficult.

An additional consideration is the question of numbers. Collections of some objects conSist of a mere few hundred items of a similar nature, but philatelic collections can contain many tens of thousands of items which are complex in nature. It follows, therefore, that looking after such a large range and number of complex objects is not a simple task.

In order to understand the magnitude of the problem it is necessary to define the specific areas which are relevant and to establish the way in which these areas are inter-related. As with the preservation of many types of objects, two basic areas have to be considered. These are:

1. *Internal factors.* The inherent properties of the individual materials; the results of their interaction; and the chemical factors arising from their individual properties, modes of manufacture and, where relevant, processing.

2. *External factors.* Temperature, relative humidity, light, pollutants, biological attack, storage, display and handling. These factors alter the rates of the natural reactions of the individual materials and/or introduce new degrading reactions.

These factors must be fully understood before any attempts can be made to establish those conditions necessary for long-term preservation of the objects concerned.

One major factor is important: time. For how long must an object or collection be preserved? The answer to this question, affects the level of importance of any individual variable involved. In most cases preservation for as long as possible is the main consideration but in trying to achieve this ideal many seemingly unimportant factors become of great importance.

From the museum and archives standpoint, there is another consideration: should the item be preserved in its original form or by some means of surrogate copy or, indeed, should the latter represent part of the process of preservation of the original. This is an important consideration for public philatelic collections as the availability of high-grade surrogate copies for researchers greatly reduces handling and its consequent effect upon condition.

4

1

The nature of the materials

Paper

Paper, the most common image support material, appears to be simple but is, in fact, extremely complex and very variable in composition. Its main constituent is a web of vegetable fibres which have been formed by a sieving action on a watery suspension of the fibres together with a range of additives which improve water absorbency and surface finish. The raw material is first processed and converted into free, single fibres which are then suspended in water and formed into a mat by the action of the papermaking mould or continuous wire mesh. Paper from the early part of the 19th century in Europe contained fibres from rags, that is cotton, linen and some hemp. Sizing agents, added to reduce the water absorbency of the sheet, consisted of gelatine or starch or alum/rosin or a combination of any two or three. As the century progressed, other fibres were introduced into the paper.

There has, in the history of papermaking, always been a shortage of suitable vegetable fibres and the quest for alternatives has been and is still very intense. Esparto grass was introduced in the 1850s, ground wood in the 1860s, chemical wood in the 1880s, for example. Modern papers are made almost wholly from wood which has been treated chemically to varying degrees to remove or reduce the lignin content and to which is then added synthetic sizing agents. It is this residual lignin present in many papers made from wood that causes one of the biggest problems in preservation. Lignin, a generic term for the brown resinous material which is deposited in thickened plant cell walls, particularly woody tissue, is decomposed by heat and light. On decomposition it produces complex strong organic acids. In addition, it absorbs atmospheric acidity, which does little for the permanence of the paper.

The presence of a mineral surface coating, usually china clay or chalk, bound together with a modified starch or co-polymers or polyvinyl alcohol and polyvinyl acetate, improves the surface quality of the paper but produces, in the main, a much weaker structure. These Art or Safety papers are a source of considerable preservation problems such as surface breakup of the coating or delamination. Allied to these coated papers are the imitation Art papers, which have no surface coating but a high percentage of mineral loading, up to 25 per cent. These papers still have a good working surface but, because of the high non fibre content do not posssess high strength or durability.

Coloured loadings, together with dyes to alter the hue of the final sheet or make it look whiter, further increase the number of variables which have to be considered. The paper may have been hand made or made by a machine producing papers of different qualities. Identifying whether a paper is hand or machine made is often difficult. Hand made paper usually has a less even distribution of fibres (sheet formation) which may be visible by transmitted light. However, the presence of a printed image on the paper will make any observations more difficult. The type of mould which is used influences the physical appearance of the paper, particularly with respect to laid and chain lines or wove in character in addition to the production of the watermark. In hand-made paper, the watermark is produced by a thinning of the paper in the areas of the mark, whilst in machine-made paper it is a compressed area.

Duplex or twin wire papers are made by pressing together two sheets of still wet paper, usually wire side to wire side, so that they unite prior to the drying stage. Thicker card material, as used for postcards, is made by uniting multiple layers of wet sheets into a compact multilayer structure. Delamination may occur under certain poor storage conditions.

When the paper has been produced there are still a number of operations which the papermarker can undertake to alter further the characteristics of the paper, the most notable one being calendering. The paper roll runs through a series of polished, heated cylinders when the paper is compressed into a thinner and more compact structure with a smoother surface. With hand made papers, pressing the sheets between heated polished metal plates produces a similar result. Papermakers of the Far East polish the paper surface, sometimes with an agate, in order to improve the surface texture.

From the first production of adhesive stamps in 1840, printers have used countless different types of paper for their reproduction, either of their choice, which was allied to the printing process to be used but, sometimes, dictated by their clients whose choice lent itself to some particular security measure which they wished to impose on the finished item. It would probably be true to say that in this specialised area of printing, far greater use of a multitude of varieties of paper has been used than in any other field of printing. Those familiar with the classic stamps of countries such as Chile, United States, Canada, Great Britain and France will appreciate this point. Whilst in some of these cases, the original designs changed little, the type of paper used changed several times. We are all familiar with the wide range of horizontally and vertically laid and wove papers. These arise from their use by the printer rather than the manufacturer of the paper and the addition of watermarks, bâtonné and quadrillé markings. Bâtonné marking consists of watermarked parallel lines and is used on both laid and wove papers. The 1871 issue of Fiji is a good example of this. The 1870 issue from the same country displays quadrillé marking, as do the 1893–94 issues of Obock. The range and variety of paper used is already well-recorded, and is sufficient to say that depending on the nature of the paper in the individual object, the object may be difficult or easy to preserve. For example if the paper is of a ground wood nature, however well that object is looked after, preservation will be difficult. Conversely a paper based on linen and cotton will present potentially fewer preservation problems. Additionally paper which has had papermakers' alum (aluminium sulphate) added with either rosin or gelatine size will be acidic, because the papermakers' alum will hydrolyse to produce sulphuric acid in the paper. Glassine, made from a well-beaten pulp, contains residual chemicals from the stock preparation. Its use is not recommended. The paper with which the objects in the collection come into contact also needs consideration, the paper of album leaves in particular. Poor album-leaf paper will deteriorate and, as it does so, cause damage to the collection which it is supposed to be preserving. Any harmful chemicals present in such album-leaf papers will migrate into adjacent philatelic items causing an almost inevitable increase in their rate of chemical deterioration. Whilst some plastic philatelic enclosures will reduce the effect of poor album leaves by reducing the migration of chemicals, none will give complete protection.

Inks

Inks may be classified into three main areas, those employed in the actual printing of the philatelic material, cancellation and writing inks. Each is quite different and each presents its own sets of problems.

Printing inks
The printing of philatelic materials can be carried out by either a letterpress (a relief process), lithography or collotype (planographic processes), line engraving or rotary photogravure (intaglio processes) techniques. Letterpress, collotype and lithography use 'paste' inks in their process. These are basically pigment based systems using a drying oil similar to linseed oil as a binding agent (vehicle) together with a number of other additives often including dyes. These inks dry by absorption into the paper and then by oxidation by the atmosphere to give a hard film. Most photogravure inks are pigment/dye based. The coloured material is dissolved in a solvent, usually one similar to xylene, together with a resin binder. Drying occurs by absorption into the paper and then by evaporation of the solvent. On evaporation, the resin dries to a film and fixes the colour to the paper. Because of the nature of these photogravure inks, there are considerably more problems with their sensitivity to organic solvents than with most other printing inks.

Stamps which have been produced by a thermographic process, for example, Turkey 1966 'Osman Faience Art' 60 k, have a raised image due to the use of a heat set powder, usually based on a pigmented polyvinyl chloride (PVC) system. The pigment powder is dusted onto the wet ink immediately after the initial printing and then subjected to infra red radiation to fuse the powder to the ink image to produce the 'engraved' finish.

Metallic printing can be produced by either a metallic ink in which the metal in a finely powdered form is used as the pigment or by foils. Identification of the method used is not always simple and often a small hand lens or microscope is necessary to make the individual identification. Metallic inks contain the metal particles distributed in a suitable vehicle. The metal 'pigment' can be silver, gold or bronze but may also be anodised aluminium. Of these two types, corrosion, discoloration and deterioration is generally less with those inks using the aluminium based metal colouring. Many of the true metals will suffer from corrosion and discoloration from a whole range of pollutants. The 1862–67, Swiss 60 centimes copper-bronze is a good example of printing using a powdered metallic ink, and an equally good example of how these inks can so easily be tarnished when exposed to pollutants.

Metallic foils consist of a thin film of usually polyester onto which has been deposited, using a vacuum technique, a thin layer of aluminium which can be anodised to almost any colour. The back of the foil has a coating of a thermoplastic adhesive, usually polyvinyl acetate (PVAc) or acrylic based, which under the heat of the foil impression stage, melts and adheres the foil to the paper. In stamp production, other foils of gold, silver, palladium and steel have been used in embossed form and backed with paper as in the case of aluminium. The first example of this technique was used in the production of the 1963 Tonga commemoratives for the first Polynesian gold coinage, which were produced by embossing gold foil backed with paper.

Cancellation inks

The important feature of cancellation inks is that they should be indelible and not be removed without causing damage to the item, rendering it unsuitable for reuse. Additionally, they should contrast with the colour of the inks used on the stamp so that they can be easily seen. Thus, the black colour of the 1840 1*d*. stamp was

9

such that the first cancellation of adhesive stamps could not be effectively carried out with a black cancellation ink, so a red ink was used. The early inks, whilst sometimes specially prepared, followed the basic traditional recipes of using a pigment suspended in a suitable medium, usually linseed oil based. The difference between these and the modern endorsing inks rests with these two ingredients, viz. the colorant and the medium. In the case of the pigmented inks, the medium remains to adhere the pigment to the surface of the paper, whilst in the case of the spirit-based inks, the medium serves to assist the diffusion of the dye colorant into the paper fibres where it remains after the medium has evaporated away. Generally, the modern dyes will show more signs of degeneration than the earlier pigments for, whilst in the latter, the medium may slowly deteriorate, it effectively protects the pigment which it coats. This will be a familiar phenomenon to those who collect early stamps and covers, and is recognisable by the brown staining around a cancellation, caused by degradation of the excess of oil medium bleeding away from the pigment. Additionally, many dyes are susceptible to light fading, which is sometimes not experienced with natural inorganic pigments. Their preservation is parallel to that required for the printed stamps upon which they appear.

The security aspect of cancellation is not always a feature of the cancellation ink, but can be in the ink or coating of the paper used in the production of the stamp. The use of fugitive inks and chalk-surfaced papers, either by accident or design, effectively prevents the reuse of stamps, as cancellations cannot be removed without serious and obvious damage to the printed design of the stamp, both inks and paper surfaces being highly sensitive to water.

Writing inks
The composition of writing inks is very varied and is dependent to a great extent on their composition and the period in which they were produced. In 'black' inks there are three main classifications: those based on carbon, iron gall and the dye systems or combinations of all three.

Historically it is the carbon ink which is encountered first. The pigment particles are ground and mixed with a gum, usually gum arabic (acacia) and often some humectant such as sugar or honey. When the ink is dry there is a thin film of carbon pigmented gum adhered to the writing surface. These are relatively simple and present very few problems apart from flaking and water solubility.

The iron gall inks form the largest group and most of the problems. The inks are produced using oak galls (oak apples), produced by a wasp on oak trees as a protection for its grubs, and copperas (iron sulphate). The galls are crushed and boiled in water to extract the tannins and copperas is then added to the resultant dark fluid to produce, after a few days exposure to the atmosphere, a 'black' ink. The production of these inks was very much a cottage industry in the 19th century and there are thousands of individual variations on the basic recipe. These inks are very strongly acidic when produced from even the simplest recipes. The addition of sulphuric acid, a common addition, to give the ink more 'bite' will increase the acid level even further, and it is not unusual to find a freshly prepared ink to have a pH of the order of 2.0. When the ink is on the paper this acidity gradually dissipates itself into the paper causing local degradation. Letters are commonly found written with this type of ink with holes in the paper caused by the ink totally destroying the paper to which it was applied. This feature is frequently encountered in early lettersheets and is all too familiar to postal historians.

The third type appeared in the 19th century and was based on dyes, related almost solely to logwood extract, which produced a blue-black ink. It was regarded as an inferior ink and was often used to adulterate the superior ink gall inks. It fades easily when exposed to light and is affected by acids and alkalis. Inks based on all three types occur very often in the published recipes of 19th century black inks. Modern black inks are made from a mixture of water soluble synthetic dyes which, in combination, produce the required black or near black colour. With the ever changing state of the dye industry, the composition of these inks is constantly fluctuating and any attempt to standardise on one type would be impossible.

Coloured inks can again be very varied. The blue inks of the 19th century are based on prussian blue pigment which can be made soluble in oxalic acid solution to produce a blue ink. More

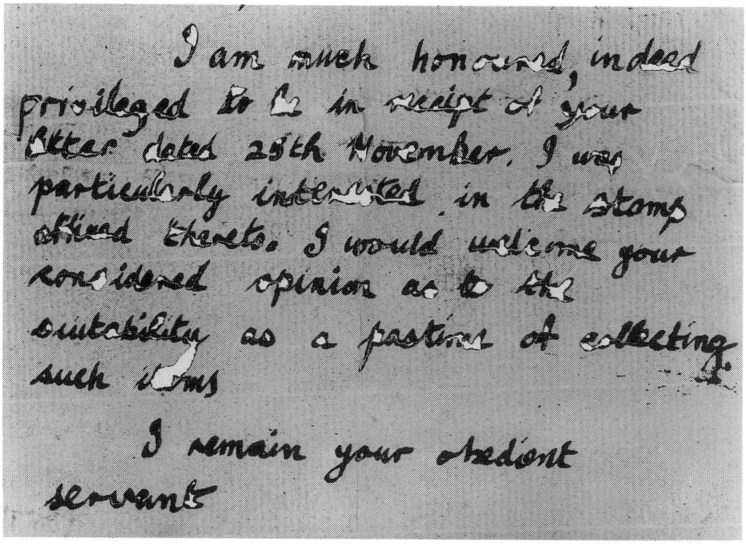
I am much honoured, indeed
privileged to be in receipt of your
letter dated 25th November. I was
particularly interested in the stamps
affixed thereto. I would welcome your
considered opinion as to the
suitability as a pastime of collecting
such items.

I remain your obedient
servant

Fig 1 The lace-work structure produced by acid ink on a letter.

recently, these and other inks have been based on modern water soluble dyes. The 19th century red inks were based on a Brazil wood extract or carmine together with a gum binding agent, whereas the modern red inks are again synthetic dye based.

The introduction in the 1940s of the ball-point pen and the fibre-tip pen of more recent times has further increased the range of writing inks. The ball-point inks are dyes, often in an almost non-drying medium, whilst the fibre pens are dyes in either water or an organic solvent medium. These inks dry by evaporation of the solvent and, because of their composition, they have a high sensitivity to a wide range of organic solvents which may occur, for example, in the form of plasticisers or monomers in some plastic storage systems.

Photographs

Photographically produced images occur in philatelic materials in some stamps and also airgraphs. The images are silver-based as in the case of the 1919 semi-official Figueroa vignette of Chile. These were sold at 5 pesos each for pre-payment of items of mail on the

Fig 2 A silver/gelatine photographic stamp,

Fig 3 Airgraphs present all the preservation problems associated with poorly processed photographs.

13

Valparaiso to Santiago flight. Iron prussiate images also occur, for example Mafeking, Cape of Good Hope 1900 1*d*. and 3*d*. The silver-based images may be present on an albumen, up to about 1900, or a gelatine base with a paper support. Many postcards have been produced in the early part of this century which are either purely photographic, based on silver and gelatine, or have photographic additions to them. Often these photographic images have been extensively hand coloured. These images are amongst the most chemically sensitive materials, being formed by minute silver particles in a filamentary or small particle state. In this state they present a very large surface area per unit volume for potential chemical attack. They can be produced from a negative using a step and repeat camera with the necessary development, fixing and washing. Any shortcomings in the fixing or the washing stages will leave behind residual chemicals. Fixer, in particular, if not properly washed out, will cause fading, discoloration and rapid loss of image. Incomplete fixing will cause image fade and staining if residual developing agents are still present in the paper. This is particularly relevant in the case of the airgraphs where speed was essential and permanence of the final document not that critical. Most of these airgraphs show varying stages of deterioration because of the inevitable short-cuts which were taken during their processing.

Hand colouring

There are a number of examples where philatelic items have had the addition of hand colouring either partially or in total, for example the illustrated envelopes of Captain Hugh Rose at the end of the 19th century. When this has occurred the colouring, which is usually in the form of a transparent wash or lines, is fairly simple in its application. Nevertheless these images present all the problems usually associated with watercolours. The colours can be either of the water soluble dye type or a transparent or near transparent pigment suspended in a gum medium. The range of coloured materials which may be encountered will be considerable and identification of such colours in this context is usually very difficult indeed: prediction of all potential problems is almost impossible. These hand-coloured items are, however, rarely encountered other than in postcards and illustrated envelopes, but hand colouring may be seen where there has been repair and retouching to items from the 19th century.

Graphite and phosphors

In England in 1957, as an experiment in automatic sorting, graphite lines were printed onto the back of postage stamps. The ink was based on a colloidal graphite with a binder and an organic solvent, drying was assisted using infra-red heaters. The lines were printed prior to the sheets being gummed, but this technique was superseded from 1959 with the introduction of fluorescent and phosphorescent lines which were printed onto the face of the stamps.

The phosphor lines are printed on top of the normal image on the stamp face by either a relief or photogravure method, the compositions of the inks, vary accordingly. A range of luminous materials have been used, the compositions of which have been changed regularly from such simple materials as zinc sulphide which was used in Australian 'tagged' stamps in 1963 to synthetic organic compounds. These zinc sulphide 'Helecon' papers include the Australian 5d. deep green, which was issued on 9 October 1963. It is one of a number of different issues which were produced on these papers. The presence of these overprinted lines may be observed using angled lighting which shows a matt finish in those areas which they cover.

The usual method of printing stripes is not universal. Some German stamps overprinted with 'lumigen', have an overprint which appears yellowish under ultraviolet light, whilst some Swiss tagged stamps are printed on a granite paper and have violet fibres present in the paper web. The Swiss phosphorescent paper was introduced on 30 November 1963 and was used for all issues.

Modern phosphors consist of an organic dye, carbazole sulphonic acid, in a base of melamine/formaldehyde unpolymerised in alcohol and water. The presence of alkalis in the phosphor ink prevent the polymerisation until the ink is printed onto the paper.

The alcohol and water evaporate and the alkali soaks into the paper. The base then dries and sets.

The presence of most ultraviolet fluorescent layers can be observed with the use of an illuminant emitting wave lengths in the range of 254 nm and between 355 and 365 nm. However materials which fluoresce outside these two main areas are used by some countries. The preservation of these coatings is a virtually insoluble preservation problem for, whilst they represent significant varieties in some of the earlier automatic sorting experiments, there are already indications of the degradation of some of the components used in the initial experiments. The major concern, however, is the long-term interactive effects of some of the components used in the coatings with the ink and/or paper.

Textiles

Philatelic items which fall into this group include stamps, some reinforced envelopes and silk inlaid postcards. The use of threads in paper dates back to 1829 when John Dickinson, the founder of the company John Dickinson and Co Ltd., introduced a method of including a variety of different threads into the body of the paper during its production. This method was later to be used in the production of the Mulready and other envelopes by that company, and in March 1841, in security experiments of stamp production. Dickinson contended that 'the protection against forgery from the introduction of threads is greater than can be derived from any printing process'. People elsewhere were of the same mind and experiments with silk threads were also carried out in France. They were used in stamp and postal stationery in Bavaria from 1849 to 1869 and also in Switzerland and Scheswig-Holstein, utilising a paper produced at Pasing Mill near Munich. Its usefulness generally ceased when these countries introduced perforating, which could be impeded by the presence of the threads.

The introduction of custom-made registered envelopes reintroduced the use of fabric in paper to provide greater strength and, thus, security for the contents, reducing the possibility of damage in the post and exposure or loss of the contents. The envelopes are

Plate 1 This envelope shows the wide range of printing, cancellation and writing inks which may be present on one item.

Plate 2 (Below left): Fibres of cotton and linen found in most 19th-century stamps.

Plate 3 (Below right): Chemical wood fibres present in a modern stamp paper.

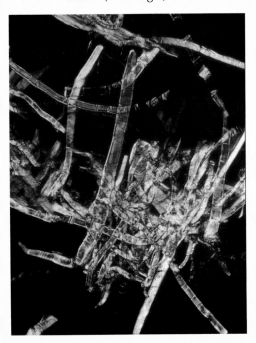

Plate 4 (Above left): Sulphide blackening of a chalk surface stamp which contained white lead. One half has been restored for comparison.

Plate 5 (Above right): Staining due to gum migration through to the front of the stamp.

Plate 6 A hand-coloured, photographic postcard having all the preservation problems associated with photographs and watercolours.

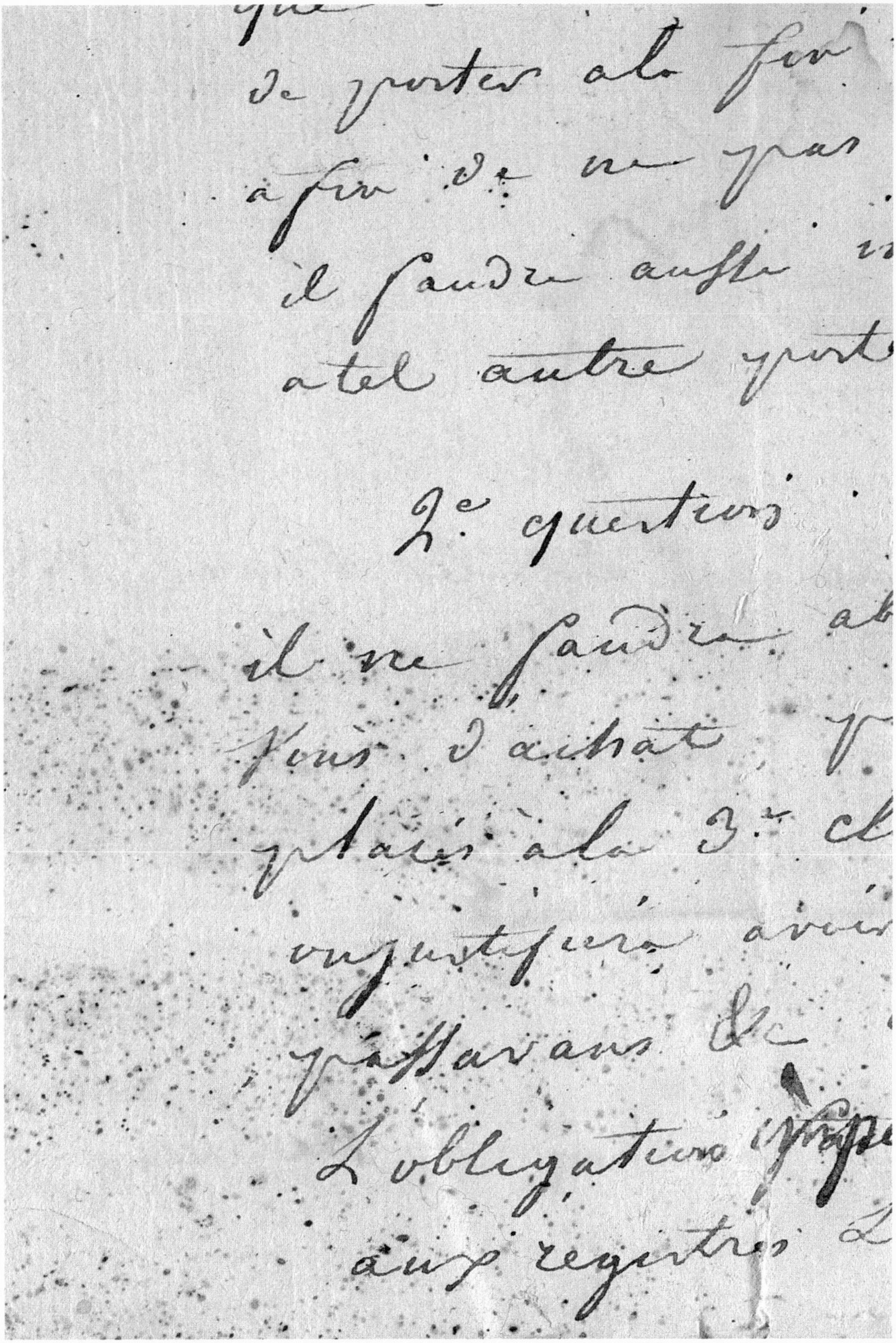
que
de porter a la fin
afin de ne pas
il faudra aussi
a tel autre port
2e question
il ne faudra ab
pour d'achat
places à la 3e cl
ou justifiera avoir
passavans &c
L'obligation
aux registres

Plate 7 Mould damage to a letter.

Plate 8 Ink transfer into an unsuitable storage plastic by the solvent action of the plastic.

Plate 9 Ink transfer on to a facing page due to lack of interleaving.

either woven fabric, usually linen, with a large percentage of white mineral loading onto which is laminated a thin layer of paper or a stout paper onto which the fabric has been bonded.

Fabrics forming part of collectable items include the silk inlays which occur in a number of postcards mainly from around the 1910s, with a printed image thereon. Silk is a very sensitive protinaceous material, attacked by a whole range of pollutants, particularly acids. Generally, it does not have a good permanence record.

Seals

Seals are another feature encountered in conjunction with some philatelic materials. They normally take one of two different forms, viz impressed wax or gummed paper. In the case of the former, fragility is the major problem and with the latter, the adhesive used for its application. The wax seals, traditionally are composed of shellac, sometimes with a little beeswax, and a pigment and are very brittle and susceptible to crumbling. Whilst they adhere well to most papers, this tends to be due to a strong surface adhesion with little diffusion of any of the components into the paper to

Fig 4 A wafer seal.

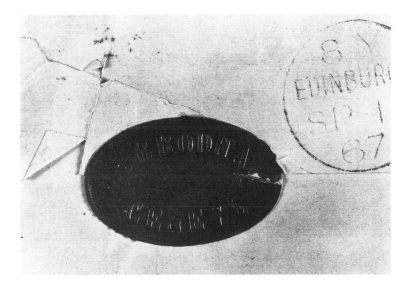

form a bond. As a result of this, damage to the seal results, usually, in surface damage to the paper at the very least. The nature of their construction makes them quite stable chemically, their preservation being dependent on the manner in which they are handled, stored and displayed. Wafer type seals are quite the reverse and present the same problems as adhesive stamps, having a variety of gums, starches, paper and printing inks used in the manufacture. They have, often, a high sensitivity to moisture and mould attack. Many applied paper seals on documents have thin lead inserts which are particularly sensitive to vapours from organic acids. The classic source of such vapours is from new oak, which should be avoided at all costs.

Adhesives

The most common adhesives used for philatelic items are gum Arabic, dextrines or polyvinyl alcohol. These widely differing substances have quite different properties.

Gum Arabic is collected from the acacia tree and cast into trays to set. It has the property to absorb water to give a sticky liquid with which we are all familiar. However, after it has been coated on to paper and dried, it is necessary that its tackiness can be recovered by the addition of moisture. To increase the effectiveness of this action, humectants, such as sugar or honey, are usually added.

Dextrines are obtained by a process of heat degradation and acid repolymerisation of starch; it is also known under the name of British gum. Because of it's mode of manufacture, it is quite often acidic in character. The adhesive properties of dextrines are generally easier to regenerate than gum Arabic, so that additives are usually less necessary. In conditions of high relative humidity, mixtures of dextrine and gelatine have been used to reduce tack at ambient temperatures in the absence of moisture. In fact, in a number of cases, adhesive formulations have been altered to allow for differing winter and summer atmospheric conditions. Additionally, various combinations of gums and dextrines have been tried including the addition of root and cereal starches.

Results of pH tests on the gums of a very wide variety of stamps has shown that most have a pH within the range of 3.8 to 5.0. Such low pH values will inevitably mean that the acid in the gums will have a deleterious effect on the stamp paper. Further, staining from gum migration through the paper of the stamp is not uncommon. There is a good preservation argument, therefore, for removing the gum from stamps but this, of course, raises ethical problems.

Pigments and dyes have been added to give a range of colours to the gum, usually as an aid to the identification of the gummed side of the paper prior to printing, when the resultant finish would have resembled that of the ungummed paper surface. This was used in particular with a blue dye added to the Australian stamps in the 1970s.

Hand or machine coating of the adhesive does not present any difficulties from the permanence point of view but the use of breakers does reduce the curl problems associated with gummed stamps. Suggestions, which may be found in published literature,

Fig 5 Gum cracking.

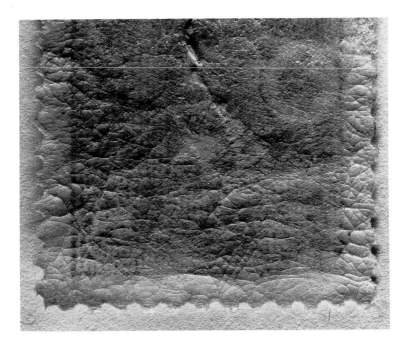

that by keeping the stamps slightly damp by the use of humectant paper with a fungicide in contact with the stamp, will help to reduce the curl. No fungicide gives permanent protection from mould so eventually, mould will grow on the 'damp' stamp. Under no circumstances should this technique be employed. It the stamp wants to curl, then the storage system should be such that it is permitted. Correct storage conditions will, however, minimise this problem.

Pressure sensitive adhesives are usually based on modified rubber or acrylics. These will all cause potential preservation problems, by migration into adjacent materials or through the material on which it is deposited, or by staining on degradation. Often all will occur. Removal of these adhesives and associated stains is extremely difficult and often impossible. Under no circumstances should pressure-sensitive tapes and papers of any type be used to carry out even a temporary repair on any philatelic item. Similar problems of staining and difficulty of removal will also occur with the use of rubber latex based gums, PVAc, and rubber based adhesives.

2

External factors affecting permanence

Temperature

Temperature relates to the degree of vibration which is present within the molecules which make up a material. The higher the temperature, the more energy the material has. When an object deteriorates, some form of chemical reaction almost always occurs and many chemical reactions are stimulated by some external energy source, the simplest of which is temperature. It follows, therefore, that there is a relationship between temperature and the rate of chemical deterioration which can occur in an object. As a general rule, the lower the temperature the slower will be the rate of the chemical reactions which cause degradation. A rise of 10°C increases the speed of most chemical reactions by a factor of about 2 or 3. The high ambient temperature of many countries will make it much more difficult to overcome this temperature effect unless some form of temperature control can be achieved.

If we are considering long term preservation of materials, the lower the temperature the slower will be the rate of deterioration and hence the longer the object will survive. However, it does not necessarily follow that the lower the temperature the better. In practice the temperature chosen must relate to the practical problems associated with low temperature storage; the preconditioning of the stored materials and their reacclimatization when they are removed from storage for use can themselves cause damage if not controlled adequately. Changes must always occur slowly and, ideally, infrequently.

Stability of temperature is also important: if large fluctuations are permitted, dimensional changes in the objects will occur. With objects which are made up of more than one basic material, and most philatelic items are complex in structure, the differing responses to temperature changes will set up physical stresses within the object with the resultant physical damage, for example, gum cracking.

Another factor affected by temperature is the rate of reproduction and metabolism of moulds, insects and animal pests. Again the general principle applies, the lower the temperature the fewer are the potential problems in these areas.

Effects of too high, low, or varying temperatures
TOO HIGH:
1. A general increase in the rate of chemical deterioration of organic materials.
2. Increased possibility of biological attack.
3. Reticulation of gums.
4. Increased curl on stamps.
5. Increased risk of reticulation of gelatine emulsions on photographs.
6. Embrittlement of paper.
7. Changes in colour of some gravure printed stamps, for example, Great Britain 1934–36.

TOO LOW:
1. Risk of condensation on objects.

VARIATIONS:
1. Physical damage due to uneven dimensional changes, for example, delamination of cards, the flaking of some writing inks, gums and pigments, cracking of gums.

The recommended archival storage temperature is 10°C, plus or minus 2°C. However, in practice, this may not be easy to achieve. It is necessary, therefore, to attain as low a temperature as possible approaching this temperature.

Relative humidity

'Humidity' is related to the water vapour which is always present in the air. The *actual* concentration of water vapour in the air is

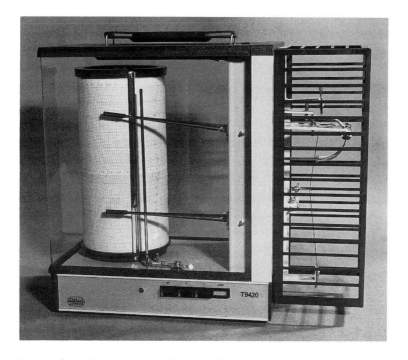

Fig 6 A thermohygrograph used to record changes in temperature and relative humidity.

measured in grammes per cubic metre and called the 'absolute humidity'. At any particular temperature the air can hold a certain maximum concentration of water vapour, a concentration which rises with temperature. This is the 'saturation value' and is again measured in grammes per cubic metre. Relative humidity is the percentage saturation of the air space for that particular temperature. That is:

Relative Humidity = Absolute Humidity ÷ Saturation Value for that temperature × 100 per cent.

The relationship between relative humidity and temperature is a very close one. Assuming there is no injection or removal of water vapour in an air space, as the temperature rises the saturation value rises and hence the relative humidity drops, and vice versa. To achieve stability in relative humidity when there are changes in

23

temperature it is necessary to have control over the absolute humidity to compensate for the changes in saturation value: some form of air conditioning is necessary which either injects water vapour into the air or removes water vapour from it.

Almost all organic materials have an affinity for water vapour, absorbing or emitting water in a vapour form from within themselves. At any particular relative humidity there is an 'equilibrium moisture content', a percentage of water held by the molecules of the material which is in equilibrium with the water vapour in the air. As the relative humidity rises so does the equilibrium moisture content and the object expands. Under the normal ranges of relative humidity in the UK, paper can have an equilibrium moisture content from about 3 to 6 per cent. This percentage will vary with the material concerned but will affect such materials as gums, inks, varnishes even though some, under normal circumstances may not always be regarded as having any association with water.

Further consideration also needs to be given to the fact that paper, in particular, rarely behaves in a uniform manner in its

Fig 7 A collection of devices used to measure relative humidity. (a) Cobalt paper strips; (b) Mason, wet and dry bulb hygrometer; (c) Whirling, wet and dry bulb hygrometer; (d) A hair hygrometer; (e) An electronic hygrometer.

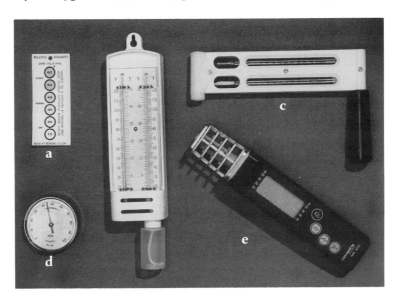

responses to changes in relative humidity. When paper is made, the fibres are not randomly orientated within the sheet; there is usually one fibre direction which predominates and this is referred to as the grain direction. With machine made papers, the grain direction is in the direction of the papermaking machine, but with handmade papers it is more difficult to define. Expansion and contraction of the paper due to changes in relative humidity can be different by up to a factor of ten with and across the grain, the cross grain direction being most affected by the changes. This will, of course, set up a differential stress pattern on any uniform material which is on the paper, for example, gums or inks.

Relative humidity is currently thought to be the main factor to affect paper permanence, a high relative humidity increasing the rate of deterioration considerably. A low, steady level, of the order of 30 per cent, will give maximum protection even if control over the other permanence factors, apart from handling, is minimal. However, in practice this is not always to achieve and maintain. A more practical recommendation, therefore, would be nearer 50 per cent relative humidity.

Effects of too high, low or varying relative humidity
Because there is such a close association with temperature, many of the deteriorating effects are similar, but it does not necessarily follow that the mechanisms of such deteriorations are the same.

TOO HIGH
1. Increased rate of deterioration of organic material.
2. Increased risk of biological damage.
3. Increased tack of gums.
4. Increased tack of some printing inks, particularly chromolithographic inks of the turn of the century.
5. Possibility of certain water soluble inks bleeding.

TOO LOW:
1. Increased temporary brittleness of paper and silk.
2. Increased temporary brittleness and cracking of gums.
3. Increase in curl problems with stamps.
4. Increase in static electricity problems.

5. Reticulation of gums, some inks, gelatine and albumen photographic emulsions.
6. Flaking of some pigments and writing inks.

1. Physical breakdown due to uneven dimensional changes.
2. Flaking of some pigments, gums, and writing inks.

Measurement of relative humidity
Instruments used to measure relative humidity fall into four main groups:

1. Colorimetric.
2. Those relying on the water vapour absorption of natural materials.
3. Those relying on water evaporation.
4. Electronic.

There are certain inorganic salts which have a particular sensitivity to the water vapour in the air, especially certain salts of cobalt. Changes in relative humidity affect the state of the water of crystallisation which causes a colour change, in the case of cobalt salts, from pink to blue. Impregnated paper strips are available which relate the colour to the ambient relative humidity. Whilst these papers are simple to use and can be put inside albums or showcases, they can give only a rough indication of the actual level of the relative humidity. Nevertheless they have their uses and do give some kind of guide and an indication if conditions are changing.

As mentioned earlier, most naturally occurring organic materials have an affinity for water vapour. Two measuring devices which capitalise on this are the hair and the paper hygrometers. With the hair hygrometer, a bunch of hair, human or horsehair, is suspended under tension from a simple lever system; as the relative humidity decreases the hair loses water and shrinks. The shrinkage causes an increase in tension which pulls the lever which in turn rotates a needle to register the relative humidity. The paper hygrometer has a coil of paper mounted onto a thin copper spiral.

The dimensions of the paper alter with changes in relative humidity but the copper does not. The tensions within the spiral therefore alter and it either winds up into a tighter coil or unwinds itself. Connection to a needle then registers the relative humidity. Both of these types read directly onto a dial but it is essential that they be calibrated against a more accurate instrument, ideally at monthly intervals, because they are notorious for not always giving consistent results; an error of 10 per cent is not uncommon. The recording type hair hygrometer is the standard instrument that is used in most museum galleries, but it is still subject to the same variability. All require regular recalibration against a whirling hygrometer.

When water evaporates, energy is required to convert the water from the liquid to vapour phase and unless there is heat energy from some external source, the temperature of the water will drop. The greater the rate of evaporation then the greater will be the drop in temperature. This principle is the one on which the Whirling hygrometer, a mobile instrument, and the Mason hygrometer, a static instrument, are based. Both instruments use two thermometers one of which has its bulb kept damp with a water-sodden wick. The wet bulb will register a lower temperature than the dry bulb. By recording the readings of the two thermometers and calculating the temperature drop of the wet bulb, reference to standard sets of tables will enable the relative humidity to be determined.

Whilst these instruments are amongst the most accurate and reliable, some care must be taken to ensure correct usage. Regrettably, manufacturers do not always supply identical thermometers for the instruments and it is essential that their readings, when dry, are identical. Because the use of the instrument relies upon the difference in readings, any original error between the two thermometers will make accurate measurement totally impossible. In both cases the wicks must be kept clean, and only distilled or deionised water should be used. The Mason hygrometer must be positioned in a place where there is a slight air draught and the correct set of tables must be used, as they differ slightly between the two instruments. For the whirling hygrometer it is important that the time of rotation, between 25 and 30 seconds, is adhered to.

Electronic devices rely either on changes in electrical capacity or electrical resistance of some form of thyrister with changes in relative humidity. The older instruments have to be calibrated each time they are used; the more modern ones have a self calibration system, but they are expensive.

Any specification for relative humidity levels must take into consideration two essential points. Firstly there is the question of microclimates; unless there is an adequate air circulation within a storage area, small pockets will occur where the ambient relative humidity can be quite different from the main mass of the air. Such pockets can occur near cooler corners or damp walls, producing conditions of high relative humidity and hence problems of which mould growth is one example. It is in conditions such as these that an electronic meter plays a very useful role because it can be used to probe local areas and microclimates easily. The second point is the accuracy to which relative humidity can be measured. Temperature can be measured very accurately but relative humidity can, for all practical purposes not be measured to a greater accuracy than plus or minus 2 per cent; in fact 5 per cent is often more realistic. There is no point, therefore, in trying to insist on very tight tolerances with the relative humidity levels recommended. It follows, therefore, that the recommended practical, storage conditions should be quoted as 50 per cent, plus or minus 5 per cent.

Light

Most philatelic items in collections are rarely exposed to light for any great length of time, but when objects are displayed or exhibited for even a short period of time, light quantity and quality become important considerations.

Chemical reactions are often stimulated by an energy injection and light is a suitable form of energy to provide this stimulation. Visible light forms part of a large range of radiations to which our eyes are sensitive only to a small part. Just beyond the visible spectrum at one end, there are the ultraviolet rays and at the other infra-red, and it is these, as well as the visible light, which have to be taken into consideration.

The highest energy levels are present in the ultra violet range reducing through violet, blue etc to the infra-red, the lowest energy level. Ultraviolet radiation is, therefore, the most damaging but infra red can cause a heating effect. Low levels of lighting must always be maintained and under no circumstances should direct sunlight be permitted to fall on the object; ideally ultraviolet light should be eliminated altogether. If tungsten filament lights, particularly spot lights, are used, it is essential that heat filters be incorporated. A rise in temperature of the object by more than 1°C over a period of ten hours is regarded as unsatisfactory.

The absorption of infra-red rays to produce heat can cause some unexpected problems, but not all materials absorb and convert infra-red equally. If, for example, the object has black and white areas, the black areas will absorb the infra-red more readily than the white, and more heat will be generated in those areas causing differential contractions within the material. This will then set up additional stresses and strains throughout the object.

It is difficult to be very precise as to how long or how much light an object may be exposed, especially if the object is not made of just one material: there are two approaches to the problem. One recommendation is that the light intensity should never rise above 50 lux, another is that the product of light intensity and exposure should be less than 500 lux. hours. This second view means that the light intensity can be permitted to rise above the 50 lux level for certain periods, as long as the overall effect over a day is essentially, on average, no more than the 50 lux level. Control of light levels is relatively simple if an exhibition is being illuminated by artificial light alone but adjustable shutters over all windows will be required to control the light levels if daylight is used. This level of lighting is low, and eyes will need time to acclimatise before full appreciation of the exhibition will be possible.

The maximum recommended level for ultraviolet light is 75 μW (microwatts) of UV per lumen of visible light, but complete absence is the only way to ensure that no damage from UV light will occur. Absence is best achieved by not using natural light to illuminate an exhibition. If this is not possible, it will be necessary to fit UV absorbent filters to all of the windows. These filters are widely available from a number of companies. By choosing the

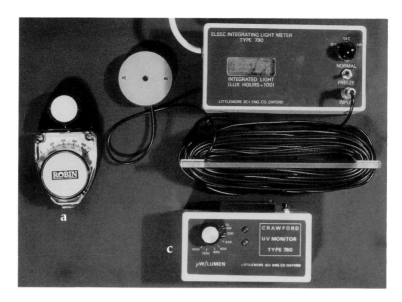

Fig 8 Instruments to measure lighting. (a) Light meter; (b) An integrating
light meter; (c) UV light meter.

correct artificial light sources, lighting similar to daylight may be
achieved without the need for filters over any of the light sources.
Fluorescent tubes are manufactured specifically to produce UV-
free, daylight quality light especially for exhibition use, for example, Philips 37.

Also associated with the effects of light is the common usage
of electrostatic paper copiers for reproduction purposes. These
machines use high intensity ultraviolet light in their action so that
potential damage is always possible. It should follow that this form
of reproduction should not be used in connection with stamps and
other philatelic materials containing light sensitive inks or dyes.
Public requests for surrogate copies of items in major institution
collections tend to be for the rare and important research items. If
these are constantly subjected to this treatment, then clearly they
will show deterioration as a result. No museum curator would
consider exposing items in his collection to unfiltered daylight, so
that exposure to the levels of ultra violet light experienced in this
machines should be unthinkable. A similar problem can be experienced with traditional photographic copying techniques. Heat and
high light intensity from photographic floodlights will cause

damage to many objects, whilst copying by flashlight is safer and there is evidence in certain non philatelic cases, where even this has been found to cause light fading of pigments after many exposures.

Problems caused by light
1. Increased rate of deterioration.
2. Yellowing of paper.
3. Embrittlement of silk.
4. Rapid deterioration of ground wood papers.
5. Fading of colours.
6. Differential expansion and contractions causing internal stresses and strains in paper, adhesives, etc.

Measuring light
1. There are a number of light meters available which are similar to photographic exposure meters, using photocells, which give a direct reading in lux of the intensity of the incident light.

2. An Integrated Light Meter designed by the Tate Gallery, London, computes the light intensity and the time for which that intensity was present. It has two readings, one of lux seconds and the other lux hours. It enables the average light intensity over a period of time to be calculated.

3. The UV light meter uses two filters and compares their transmissions, using internal photocells to assess the proportion of UV light compared with the visible light incident upon the meter. It registers the proportion as microwatts of UV per lumen of visible light.

Biological factors

Moulds
Whilst attack of philatelic items by mould often occurs, there are certain conditions required for mould to infest and without these conditions being correct, mould attack cannot occur. There are many moulds but not all of them can attack paper or associated materials.

In considering moulds there are a number of factors which have to be understood. Firstly, normal air is laden with mould spores of a great variety, which are constantly searching for a host and for the correct conditions to reproduce. A sterile object can become infested in seconds and even if an object is not mould-infested, it will still be covered with latent spores waiting for the conditions to become satisfactory.

The climatic conditions which aid mould reproduction are varied, but a relative humidity below 65 per cent and a temperature below 18°C will not permit the reproduction of most of the common moulds which can cause preservation problems. Mould, experiencing conditions below these, will either stay dormant below relative humidity of 65 per cent, or reproduce only slowly below 18°C, and will eventually die. The main controlling factor is, however, relative humidity.

Moulds reproduce themselves by first finding the correct conditions for reproduction, setting up centres where webs of whispy mycelium are produced. When the colony reaches maturity, the spore sacs burst and release thousands of microscopic spores which, once air borne, search out suitable sites to begin the reproductive cycle all over again.

Moulds need water, food and trace elements to reproduce, but their requirements are small. Sufficient food can often be transmitted from a finger print. With philatelic items, food for mould can be split into two main areas. Only a few varieties of mould will degrade cellulose, the most common being *Chaetonium glubosum*, whereas most degrade the size in the paper, especially gelatine, also any starch or sugars present in the gums. Of the many trace elements required, the main one is iron which is commonly present as an adulterant in paper and many other materials. Of these requirements, water is the most essential and also the easiest to control by maintenance of the recommended relative humidity levels. Another factor which needs to be taken into consideration is the number of changes of air and air flow. Mould prefer static or near static air conditions, for example next to walls and behind storage units where microclimates can be formed by stagnant air. It must be appreicated, however, that these microclimates can still occur even with full air conditioning. It is essential, therefore, that some slight air circulation should be incorporated within any long term storage arrangement.

Moulds on philatelic items can show themselves in two main ways. Large heavily coloured deposits can be produced by varieties of, for example, *Aspergillus* and *Penicillium*. The smaller spots, reddish brown in colour, often referred to as 'foxing', are of unknown source and are still undergoing much research. Microclimates can actually be created by materials such as certain gums and some additives. If sugar or honey has been added to adhesives to give them better working properties, higher moisture levels can be produced locally, with the increased chance of conditions being correct for mould growth. Both sugar and honey have the property of being able to absorb moisture from the atmosphere and raise the moisture levels locally because of their humectant properties.

When collections have become affected by mould damage it is essential that the reproductive cycle be stopped to ensure that no further damage takes place. The mould will have developed because the material has become damp or been stored in too high a relative humidity, immediate action must be taken. If the quantities are large, then the individual items should be wrapped in polythene bags and frozen in a deep freeze. This stops any further damage and gives time to organise a proper rescue plan where the items can be dealt with one by one without haste.

Fumigation will destroy any living mould on an object but there are risks in using most fumigants, either to the operator or the object. Additionally, no fumigant, which is safe to the object, can give more than a limited period of protection so it can never be regarded as a substitute for correct storage conditions. With items which have mould problems on them, the first essential is to dry them out. This is often a slow process but essential. When the object is dry it should be taken out of doors and the dried surface mould be dusted off the object. It is essential that the mould spores are not inhaled as this, in some people, may cause respiratory problems.

The value of philatelic items is considerably affected by condition and if a stamp has mould damage its value will be very much reduced. Removal of the offending stain may restore the object to near pristine condition. However, the treatments recommended are much more difficult to carry out than inferred by some published instructions. Even recommended solvents and bleaches can cause problems or damage which can either have immediate effect or become apparent over a period of time. When restoration is essential, and this raises the ethical problem, it should be carried out only by an expert.

Insects

There is a close relationship between mould and insect infestation as most insects prefer climatic conditions similar to those suitable for mould reproduction, and for many insects mould is their food. The range of insects which may be encountered will be very variable, some causing damage in the adult stage but others at the larval stage only. The damage usually occurs as a burrowing action, usually of the larvae through the paper, board or leather bindings, and there can be further problems caused by the insect excrement which can also cause damage.

Windows should not be left open at night, and surfaces of floors and shelves should not have cracks in which potential food may collect or insects harbour. Regular cleaning and dusting is important as dead insects can act as foodsources for others. There should be no eating or drinking in the area in which the collection is stored and animals such as cats and dogs should be excluded as hair and excretions can provide ample food for many insects. Most of this damage can be prevented by relatively simple means and can be summed up as good housekeeping.

If objects have become affected, then there is the problem of disinfection. There are insecticides which can be used, but these always present some problem either to the user, or potential damage to the object. However, recent research has shown that wrapping the objects in polythene bags and freezing them at $-30°C$ for three days kills the insects at all stages of development causing very little, if any, damage to the object or the user. Shelves may be decontaminated and further protected by using insecticidal lacquers along the very backs of the shelves. These lacquers do not come into contact with the objects stored on them so can cause no harm and are readily available from the local pharmacist.

Rodents

Mice and rats can cause undue damage to collections but methods of control are fairly well established. If a collection is housed in a steel cabinet then, obviously, the chances of attack will be greatly reduced. Again it is a matter of good housekeeping to ensure that the collection is not put at risk.

Pollutants

Chemical contamination of philatelic items from some external source is a major affecting deterioration. Sources are not only limited to the atmosphere, but include materials which are used for storage, display or with which the collection is brought into contact for some other reason. Consideration has, therefore, to be given to all these forms of pollution, irrespective of source.

Many pollutants from the atmosphere will be quite familiar to you, and may be classified into two groups, the gaseous and the particulates. The common gaseous pollutants include sulphur dioxide and hydrogen sulphide, and are derived mainly from the burning of fossil fuels. Sulphur dioxide is an acid gas which under

Fig 9 Rodent attack on a stamp album.

gentle oxidising conditions is converted to sulphuric acid with its well established corroding effects. It causes a darkening and embrittlement of paper and, in the case of albums, concentrates around the edges which are more exposed to atmospheric pollution. Hydrogen sulphide gas will cause tarnish and fading of silver-based photographic images, tarnishing of bronze printing inks and darkening of pigments which contain lead white.

Other gaesous pollutants include the oxides of nitrogen which can originate from car exhausts, burning natural gas, or from degrading cellulose nitrate plastic which may be present as lacquers on some philatelic items and even storage materials. These are oxidised to nitric acid, an acid which is more corrosive and damaging than even sulphuric acid. This acid will degrade, by oxidation and acid attack, almost any organic material and, additionally, many pigments and dyes and photographic images.

Ozone, a very powerful oxidising agent, can originate from a number of sources. It is formed by many electrostatic copying machines, and some electrostatic dust precipitators in air-conditioning systems, but one of the main sources is the effect of sunlight on car exhaust gases. The level of reactivity of ozone is such that it has a short life, and it will react very rapidly with most

Fig 10 Drager tubes used to measure the concentrations of gaseous pollutants.

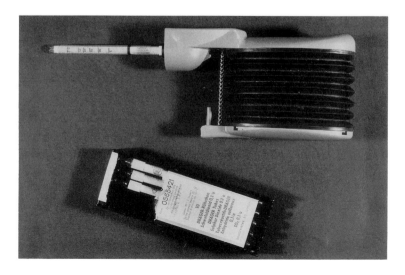

organic materials increasing the rate of deterioration. A further potential source of pollution is ammonia from dye line copiers which can affect photographic images and some pigments.

Specialist equipment is available to measure the levels of these gases in the atmosphere. The equipment consists of a small air pump which draws air though a tube containing a chemical which changes colour gradually down the length of the tube as the concentration increases, rather like the 'Breathalizer' tubes used by the police to measure the concentration of alcohol vapour on the breath. Various tubes are available to measure the concentrations of specific gases, and this equipment is manufactured by Drager in West Germany.

Special activated carbon filters and granules are available to absorb these gaseous pollutants and these may be used to clean incoming air, or be placed in storage boxes to protect the contents. There is, however, one difficulty with their use because there is no simple way to be sure that they are still active after a period in operation.

Particulates, i.e. solid particles suspended in the air, can have a very much more varied composition depending on local conditions and may be animal, vegetable or mineral in origin. The particle sizes range from 0.01 micrometers for smog and tobacco smoke to 100 micrometers for pollens. Not all of these 'dusts' will be equally black; dust from salts from evaporated water and cement, for example, will be whitish. Probably the worst offender is the domestic open fire and dusts originating from the burning of fossil fuels, fly ash, which can cause acid damage to objects on which they settle. Good housekeeping is again essential with any form of collection and maintenance of a clean air condition, free from dust, is required, not only to reduce any chemical attack, but to make the environment less attractive to mould, insects and rodents.

The removal of all of these dusts in the air is difficult requiring highly specialised filters to remove this very wide range of particles. Nevertheless, if a collection is regarded as being of real value, procedures will have to be adopted to ensure at least 95 per cent removal of the total weight of dust across the particle size range from the incoming air. This is, however, only possible with a full air filtering system. Electrostatic dust precipitators are another effective form of dust extraction. These have an array of wires which are charged to a high electrical potential but, whilst being efficient, they have the disadvantage of producing ozone gas. Its oxidising properties will, in addition to causing deterioration, convert the sulphur dioxide in the air into sulphuric acid.

Pollutants in the form of migratory chemicals from adjacent mounting, storing and display materials can come from seemingly innocent sources, the main ones being paper, board, adhesives and plastics. Because of this, it is essential that detailed material analysis information is made available by the manufacturers to support any claim that their product is safe for the long-term storage of philatelic items.

The problems associated with paper and board may be grouped together and relate mainly to their modes of manufacture and composition. The worst ones arise from the use of mechanical or ground wood. The problems associated with this fibre type have already been described and the identification test details are in the Appendix. All give a simple indication of their presence in the yellowing of the paper and board together with an embrittlement. This embrittlement can cause physical damage to materials supported by it. Unless handled very carefully, the board or paper can fracture and split apart the object mounted on it. Additionally, the acid which is created and absorbed by these fibres, or more precisely the lignin which they contain, also migrate into adjacent, good quality paper, card and board and cause them to suffer the effects of acid degradation. Further acidity due to the use of papermakers' alum used in the paper or board manufacture can generate acid which can also migrate into adjacent materials.

Hydrogen sulphide as well as occurring naturally can be emitted from a number of materials which may be found in association with philatelic items, particularly under acid conditions. The range is wide including many papers, rubbers, textiles, pigments, dyes, mounting and display boards and adhesives. One major problem is that reduceable sulphur can be dormant in a material. As the material becomes acidic, by absorption of acid from the atmosphere for example, conditions can be created to make the reduceable sulphur active and create hydrogen sulphide.

The damage which can be caused has already been described and there are tests to determine the potential reduceable sulphur problem in a material, details of which are given in the Appendix.

Certain varnishes, bleached woods and adhesives which have had hardeners added as setting agents, can exude peroxides into adjacent materials. These oxidising agents will cause degradation of many organic materials. Woods, in particular new oak, for example, can emit organic acid vapours which will attack many metals but in particular lead which may be present in certain types of document seal. Unfortunately there is not a test at present to detect the small quantities of oxidising agents these materials emit. The best recommendation is to avoid such materials which, because of the make up, have the potential to cause this particular problem.

pH and acidity

Throughout this book acidity and pH have been shown to be major factors associated with the deterioration of philatelic materials. The terms pH, acidity and alkalinity can refer only to materials which are soluble in water or are already aqueous solutions. In fact water is the key. Without the presence of water, the concepts of pH, acidity and alkalinity cannot exist.

Pure water is taken as the standard for neutrality. Water molecules can break down into ions (electrically charged particles) hydrogen ions which are positively charged and hydroxyl ions which are negatively charged. But only a very small percentage by water is taken as the standard for neutrality, if the concentration of hydrogen ions of 0.0000001 grams per litre. If an acid is added to water it produces hydrogen ions of its own which increase the concentration of hydrogen ions to, say, 0.01 grams per litre. If an alkali is added it depresses further the number of water molecules which ionise so that the concentration of hydrogen ions drops from the already low figure to, say, 0.0000000000001 grams per litre. The concentration of hydrogen ions produced by water is taken as the standard for neutrality, if the concentration is higher than this the solution is an acid, if lower an alkali.

Working with such very small figures is, however, very tedious so a scale was devised so that mathematically these figures were converted to more manageable numbers. This scale is the pH scale. On this scale water, which has a hydrogen ion concentration of 0.0000001 grams per litre, has a pH of 7.0, acid with a hyrogen ion concentration of 0.0001 grams per litre a pH of 4.0 and an alkali with a hydrogen ion concentration of 0.0000000001 grams per litre a pH of 10. The scale is a logarithmic one and is defined as the negative logarithm to the base ten of the hydrogen ion concentration of an aqueous solution. In practice it means one more than the number of 0s after the decimal point before arriving at the digit, assumed in this example to be 1, gives the pH. Because it is a negative logarithm the number goes down as the acidity goes up. It means, therefore, that between a pH of 4.0 and 5.0 there is a factor of ten, the pH 4.0 being the more acid and similarly a pH of 12.0 is 1000 times more alkaline than pH 9.0. On this scale, a change of 0.3 is equivalent to an acidity or alkalinity change by a factor of 2.

In real terms solutions can have pHs ranging from about -1.5 for a very strong acid to about 14.5 for a very strong alkali. In practice, however, the most useful range is usually between 0 and 14. the pH of solutions may be measured using special electronic probes or by the affect of changes in colours of selected dyes called indicators: details of these tests are given in the Appendix.

3

Storing and mounting the collection

Storage materials

Album leaves

Most collectors regard the leaves of their albums which support the stamps in one way or another as being permanent, but this is a claim that can rarely be met by exising album-leaf papers. Commercially, no album leaf exists which is archivally stable regardless of their cost. Whilst some will last for many years, others will have a relatively short useful life. Leaves can be manufactured with good permanence properties which will also guarantee that no pollutants of any kind will be present to migrate into adjacent stamps. However, it is questionable whether it is always necessary to have leaves of the very highest degree of purity. Whilst not ideal, the use of polyester or polyolefin stamp protectors will reduce any attack by chemicals in the album leaf paper migrating into the stamps. The protection given by such protectors, though, cannot be guaranteed.

If leaves are to have archival qualities they should conform to the following specifications.

1. All should be free from lignin.
2. All should have a pH between 6.0 and 8.5.
3. All should be free from reduceable sulphur.
4. All should be free from aluminium sulphate.
5. All paper should have a soft non-abrasive surface.

The specifications for storage boxes should conform to numbers 1, 2 and 3.

The following are the results of tests carried out on 11 commercially-available album leaves.

1. With one exception, all had a pH of between 4.5 and 4.8
2. The one exception to the low pH had a pH of 6.0 but contained lignin, as did one other paper.
3. All contained aluminium sulphate.
4. All failed the silver tarnish test for reduceable sulphur.
5. All contained iron compounds.
6. One had a PVC stamp protector under which the paper had a pH of 3.8.
7. One had a polystyrene stamp protector which failed the solvent activity test.
8. All were made from fibres which were obtained from a mixture of chemically extracted hard and soft woods.

The conclusion reached is that none of these album leaves was suitable for long-term, archival mounting of philatelic materials.

Archivally suitable album leaves, meeting all the specifications, will soon be available for collectors. The ideal leaf should be made of paper which is 100 per cent cotton linters with a pH 6.5 to 7.5 and a modern synthetic sizing agent, for example, 'Aquapel'. Such papers already exist.

The use of glassine gummed hinges cannot be recommended, for reasons already given (see pages 7 and 8). The paper has the property of retaining processing chemicals only to release them later for migration into adjacent materials. The gum is acidic, again with conservation problems. Further there is the damage caused to the back of the stamp. Stamps in original condition can no longer be so described once stamp hinges have been used. It is a much better conservation practice to use plastic stamp protectors made of the correct polymer.

Glassine stock books may cause damage to the philatelic materials stored in them. However, bearing in mind that items are not stored in this material for long periods, its continued use in this manner should not cause any preservation problems.

Plastics
The use of stamp and leaf protectors together with enclosures for postcards and documents are now widely used but care in selection of the correct product is essential.

Plastics, when used for conservation storage, have problems of their own. To many people all plastics materials appear the same but their variety is enormous. Many contain external plasticisers, which act as molecular lubricants and are incorporated into the plastic's manufacture to increase the flexibility of the plastics in sheet form. These external plasticisers can volatilise and cause the plastic to become brittle or migrate into adjacent material where they can act as solvents for many inks, particularly gravure printing inks, ball-point and felt-tip pens and typewriter inks. Polyvinyl chloride plastics, which are commonly sold for the storage of stamps, postcards first-day covers, etc. are amongst the worst offenders. In addition to the plasticiser problem, PVC degrades to emit acid gases which can migrate into adjacent materials. Under no circumstances should PVC be used for any long or even short term storage. It is to be regretted that PVC is still the major plastic being offered by many philatelic sources for storage of stamps, first-day covers and postcards.

The use of polystyrene-based plastics for stamp mounting also gives some cause for concern. It is possible for the monomer, styrene, to be emitted by the plastic which can act as a solvent on certain types of inks.

In the Appendix there are details of tests to identify PVC, and to evaluate the solvent activity of plastics to assess their suitability for long-term storage.

All plastic storage materials will create a static electricity problem to varying degrees of seriousness. Some plastics are sold with an anti-static coating which can dissolve the inks from stamps stored in them. At least one product on the market uses this type of coating on a 'safe' plastic so destroying the good conservation properties of that material. There have been suggestions of using humectant materials within the plastic enclosures to raise the relative humidity locally and hence reduce static. These will cause mould problems and are, therefore, not acceptable.

Nitrate film has been used in the past for the storage of some philatelic items. Most of these items by now will have fallen to dust because of the emission of nitrogen dioxide gas from the plastic. Apart from its additional fire risk, this plastic must never be used for the storage of any object.

The plastics industry is changing very rapidly, so it is difficult to ensure the continued quality of all materials. A very varied and wide range of additives, which may or may not include plasticisers, can be used by the manufacturer who is usually unwilling to divulge those present in a particular plastic. Further, because most manufacturers do not quote any conservation specifications for their products, they are free to change the quality of the product without any announcement. As the conservation requirements are much more stringent than for any other usage and the market is small, it is often difficult to find suitable conservation storage materials. Regular testing on an empirical basis of batches is the only sure way to ensure the continued conservation quality of the plastics being used unless the manufacturer is prepared to give written conservation guarantees.

Any plastics which are going to come into intimate contact with philatelic items should conform to the following specifications:

1. They should be free from chlorinated compounds.
2. They should be free from external plasticisers.
3. They should be free from solvent activity.
4. They should have a non-abrasive surface.

Ten samples of commercially available stamp protectors, some of which claimed archival quality, have been examined. The results were:

1. One of these was PVC.
2. Six were polystyrene most of which failed the solvent activity test.
3. Two were polyester but one had an anti-static coating on it which failed the solvent activity test.
4. One had a paper backing which failed the reduceable sulphur test.
5. One was of a polyolefin composition.

At present there is really only one type of stamp protector commercially available which is of polyester composition with a safe pressure sensitive adhesive backing that is archivally satisfactory; the polyolefin one will be chemically safe but will offer less physical protection.

Of the plastic album leaf protectors available, most are polystyrene, some PVC, but safe polyester protectors are available from a few manufacturers. However, plastic album-leaf protectors can increase the effect of pollutants from the album-leaf paper if the leaf paper is not archivally safe. Because the pollutants will be trapped inside the protector they will not be able to diffuse away into the air. Hence, attack by these pollutants on the items stored within them is more likely to occur.

Of the commerically available first-day cover protectors and postcard protectors most are made from PVC and many are definitely unsuitable for even short-term storage. Polyester protectors for both are commercially available.

Mounting for exhibition

Any exhibition of philatelic items must ensure that the display conditions conform to those described earlier. Additionally, there are important factors to be considered relating to the actual mounting and framing of the exhibits. If individual stamps are to be exhibited, they must be mounted on a paper sheet by one of the types of protectors acceptable for conservation purposes.

Mounting boards come in a great variety of colours and qualities, most of which are not suitable for use in conservation. Most have centres containing ground wood which will cause migration damage. Many dyes and pigments added to colour boards emit compounds which will deteriorate a wide range of images. It is essential, therefore, that any mounting should use conservation quality board, conforming to the specifications laid down earlier for album leaf paper. The safest boards are made from cotton linters, often sold as 'rag' boards, without any dyes or pigments added. These boards are manufactured for the conservation mounting of prints, drawings and watercolours.

Pressure-sensitive tapes used to adhere the object to the mounting board should not be used, again for reasons stated earlier. Either a good quality starch paste or one based on methyl cellulose should be used in conjunction with Japanese paper to produce the necessary hinges for mounting.

The use of a bevelled window mounting style, where there is an overlay of mounting board in which is cut an aperture, will give maximum protection and flexibility of artistic presentation. Most types of backing boards used in framing will cause chemical migration problems into the back of the item being displayed. Whilst there are 'safe' backing boards available, it is simpler and a lot more convenient if a chemical barrier is placed behind the mounted item and in front of the backing board. This will stop the possibility of any contaminants migrating through to the framed item. Of the chemical barriers available, the safest, cheapest and easiest available is aluminium foil which is used in the kitchen. The use of this material will even permit the continued use of the old wooden backing boards which are responsible for most of the 'wood burn' staining on the front and back of many prints and watercolours.

If there is a risk of ultraviolet radiation from any source, the framed item may be further protected if a thin sheet of UV polycarbonate is positioned immediately behind the glass. This thin protective sheet is almost invisible and gives added protection, because it is virtually unbreakable. If the frame is dropped and the glass broken, the polycarbonate sheet will ensure that no glass fragment damages the exhibit. Further it will give security protection for the exhibited item.

Health and safety

Whilst this book is concerned with the preservation of items in a collection, it is important that some consideration be given to the hazards associated with some of the chemicals and techniques used by philatelists. Restoration techniques should not be practised by the amateur so contact with a wide range of bleaches and stain-removing chemicals does not fall within the confines of this publication. However, other chemicals and techniques are used to facilitate detailed examination of many objects.

The two most common organic solvents encountered, which

are used to help identify watermarks, are benzene and benzine. Whilst there is little difference in their spelling, and they are often even pronounced the same, there are considerable chemical differences. Benzene is flammable and extremely toxic, even in very small quantities, being absorbed through the skin as well as by inhalation and ingestion. It causes blood cancer, and must *never* be used for philatelic purposes. Benzine is a petroleum ether obtained from the distillation of oil. It is also flammable, but as long as the vapours are not inhaled, it is safe to use within the context of philately. Confusion must be avoided between these two solvents.

Carbon tetrachloride is another organic solvent which is used by philatelists. It is not flammable but is toxic by skin absorption, inhalation and ingestion. It causes severe liver damage in addition to being carcinogenic. In the presence of a naked flame, the vapour can be converted into phosgene which can cause rapid damage to the victim even after a short exposure. Phosgene has been used in gas warfare. A much safer organic solvent which has similar properties to carbon tetrachloride is 1.1.1. trichloroethane, which is much more suited to its use in philately. It is available commercially in small quantities.

Solutions are sold commercially to ease in the removal of stamps from envelopes, etc. Whilst most of these are safe to use, caution should always be exercised.

It has been stated that if any chemical were handled as if it were ink, the user would come to little harm, and this approach is to be commended.

A very useful tool for the philatelist is the ultraviolet light, available in a variety of forms. Long and short wavelength sources of UV are used, and both can be damaging to the eyes, the shorter wavelengths being more damaging. If used sensibly within the guidelines laid down by the manufacturer, no harm should come to the user, but it is essential to be aware of the potential dangers.

One further potential hazard which has already been mentioned in the text is the inhalation of dry mould when dusting off infected material. Suitable dust masks are available to ensure that no respiratory problems will occur.

Philately is not a hazardous pastime: there are only a very few potential dangers, but they still must not be ignored.

Conclusions

Collections, whether large or small, have been accumulated through many hours of dedication and often considerable expense. It is poor economic policy not to protect one's investment by not using safe environmental conditions and materials. It is regrettable that, for many years, the philatelic business has not directed ifself towards preserving collected items. Compared with the conservation of other objects based on paper, the philatelic world is years behind. However, there has, over the last few years, been some interest shown in the correct choice of materials and conditions for long-term preservation. But there is still a long way to go.

It is hoped that this book will not only inform the reader of recommended ways to ensure the longevity of items in his or her collection, but also the reasons for concern. The responsibility lies with the collector to ensure that the items within his or her care are protected for the future.

Appendix

Glossary

Further Reading

Appendix: scientific tests

Tests for the presence of:

Lignin One drop of phloroglucinol in alcohol is added to the paper and then one drop of concentrated hydrochloric acid. A magenta colour indicates the presence of lignin.

Reduceable sulphur Silver tarnish test. The test involves placing an acidified sample of paper, board or adhesive on to the surface of a small piece of highly polished silver. The sample and silver are incubated at a high humidity at 80°C for three periods of eight hours. Any sign of coloration or tarnishing on the silver mirror surface indicates the presence of reduceable sulphur. A more detailed procedure was first published by Collings and Young in *Studies in Conservation*, 21, (1976), pp. 79–84.

Organic chlorides in plastics The Beilstein test. A short length of thin copper wire is heated in a flame (a gas lighter will often do) until no colour is imparted to the flame. The hot wire is then touched onto the plastic and reintroduced into the flame. A green colour in the flame indicates the presence of organic chlorides. Polyvinyl chloride plastics all give a positive result.

Aluminium sulphate (papermakers' alum) In a fume cupboard one drop of an ammonia/tartarate solution is added to the paper and left to soak in. One drop of a quinalizarin in pyridine and acetone is added followed by two drops of ethanoic acid. A negative result gives a pinkish coloration. Any suggestion of blue indicates the presence of aluminium. Details of this test were first published by Collings in 'Resins in Conservation', *Proceedings of the Scottish Society for Conservation and Restoration*, (Edinburgh 1982), pp. 7–7 and 7–8.

Solvent activity test The plastic under test is placed in contact with a stamp, ideally gravure printed, under slight pressure. It is incubated at a temperature of 80°C for five days after which the plastic is examined. Any sign of an ink transfer into the plastic shows that something in the plastic has a solvent action on the stamp. Details of this test were first published by Collings in 'Resins in Conservation', *Proceedings of the Scottish Society for Conservation and Restoration,* (Edinburgh 1983), pp. 7–3 and 7–4.

Iron compounds One drop of concentrated hydrochloric acid is added to the paper or board and followed by one drop of an aqueous solution of ammonium thiocyanate. A red coloration indicates the presence of iron compounds.

pH If it is possible to destroy part of the material under test, for example, album-leaf paper, the method is as follows: One gram of the material is broken up and supended in $70 \, cm^3$ of boiled distilled water for one hour. The pH of the aqueous extract is then measured with a previously calibrated pH probe and meter.

If a non-destructive method needs to be employed then one drop of cold boiled distilled water is added to the surface of the material, left for 30 seconds and the pH of the residual surface solution measured using a surface pH electrode, recording the value when the pH is stable or near stable. This method cannot give as reproduceable results as the aqueous extract method and is accurate only to the nearest 0.3 pH units at the best.

Glossary of some materials and preservation terms

Absolute Humidity The concentration of water vapour present is in an air space expressed in grams per litre.

Catalyst A substance which alters the rate of a chemical reaction without being used up in the reaction

Co-polymer A plastic or adhesive which has been manufactured using two different monomers, polymerised together.

Deckle The irregular, feathered edge of a sheet of hand made paper.

Dye A coloured substance which is soluble in the supporting medium.

Glassine A thin translucent paper made from well beaten paper fibres.

Humectant A substance which has the ability to absorb moisture from the air or to give out moisture to the air depending on relative humidities.

Hydrolysis The decomposition of compounds by interaction with water, alone or in the presence of acids or alkalis or the formation of an acid and a base by the interaction of a salt with water.

Laid Paper structure formed on a mould which has horizontal and vertical wires on it, imparting this pattern into the paper.

Lignin A complicated mixture of substances formed by certain plant cells and deposited in thickened cell walls, particularly woody tissue.

Loading Mineral additives in paper giving the sheet a smoother surface and greater opacity.

Lumen The unit of luminous flux given as the amount of light energy emitted per unit solid angle per second by a source of intensity of one international candle.

Lux A unit of the illumination produced by light from a source of one international candle falling normally on a surface at a distance of one metre.

Migration The movement of molecules from one material into another or to the surface of the material in which they are contained.

Monomer A small, simple molecule, which can either unite with itself or other small molecules and form much larger molecules called polymers.

Oxidation A chemical reaction where oxygen is added, or a decrease in electronegativity of the material.

Pigment A coloured material which is insoluble.

pH The negative logarithm to the base ten of the hydrogen ion concentration of aqueous solutions.

Photodegradation The action of light energy stimulating chemical reactions.

Plasticizer An additive to polymers which acts as a lubricant for the long chain molecules to increase the flexibility of the polymer.

Polymerisation A chemical reaction involving the joining up of numbers of small molecules into very large molecules.

Reduction A chemical reaction involving the removal of oxygen or an increase in electronegativity of the material.

Relative Humidity The ratio of absolute humidity and saturation value for that temperature expressed as a percentage.

Rosin A natural resin obtained from certain pine woods.

Saturation Value The maximum concentration of water vapour an air space can hold at that particular temperature, expressed in grams per litre.

Solvent A liquid which has the ability to dissolve other materials and form a solution.

Wove A paper structure which has been formed on a mould made from woven wire or fabric, without the lines associated with laid paper.

Further reading

Baynes-Cope, A. D. *Caring for books and documents* (The British Library, 1989)

 'Mould stains on stamps' *Stamp Collecting*, vol. 114 no. 24, August 1970

Baynes-Cope, A. D. and Collings T. J., 'Some specifications for materials and techniques used in the conservation of archives' *Journal of the Society of Archivists*, vol. 6, no. 6, October 1980, pp 384–386

B.S. 5454, *Recommendations for the storage and display of archival documents* (1977)

Collings. T. J., *Archival care of still photographs* Information Leaflet No. 2; Society of Archivists, 56 Ellin Street, Sheffield S1 4PL

 'A web for words' *Inside Science No. 14; New Scientist*, 5 November 1988

 'Preserving your collection', *Stamp Magazine*, vol. 54, nos. 10 and 11, October and November 1988

Hunter, D., *Papermaking* (Dover, New York, 1978)

Kindley, A. D., 'Medical hazards in philately' *London Philatelist*, vol. 89

Nol, Lea, Henis, Y. and Kenneth, R. G., 'Biological factors of foxing in postage stamp paper'. *International Biodeterioration Bulletin* 19(1); Spring 1983

Nolan, C. E., 'Philatelic Preservation', *American Philatelist*, vol. 93, nos. 3, 5; vol. 96, no. 5

Schoolley-West, R. F., 'Philatelic Conservation', *Library Conservation News*, nos. 13 and 14, October 1986 and January 1987

Thomson, G., *The Museum Environment* (Butterworths, 1978)

Williams, L. N. and M, *Fundamentals of Philately* (American Philatelic Society, State College, Pennsylvania, 1971)